This book is dedicated
to all those standing on
Psalm 46:10
BE STILL & KNOWN
THAT I AM GOD

Acknowledgments

I want to thank each lady that took time to prepare a devotion for this book to encourage those that will pick this book up.

I pray this book will bring you a strong message of love that will be true and unconditional. Not only will you feel the love of God in your heart, but you will also feel true love that we share with you thur our testimonies. I pray you are blessed by this book.

With much love,

Angela Thomas Smith

TABLE OF CONTENT

ANGELA THOMAS SMITH

Standing Strong Through The Storm
Scripture:
Hebrews 11:1 Now Faith is the substance of things hoped for, the evidence of things not seen.
Words of encouragement
Faith is defined in dictionary as the complete trust of confidence in someone or something. A strong belief in God or in the doctrine of a religion, based on spiritual apprehension rather than proof.
Faith is also an action word, one can't except God to drop things from the sky. Example you trusting God for a job , but If you never go job hunting you cant active faith. Word of God states faith without works is dead.
Father God 1 thank you for yet another day that was not promised us, but you extended your grace in mercy more time for us to get it right.

women that
pray together stay
together.

Daughter Of The Living God, You Are Blessed!

Suddenly, there was a massive earthquake and the prison was shaken to its foundations. All doors immediately flew open and the chains of every prisoner fell off.

Acts 16:26

Spirit of the living God, 1 bow before You today. 1 ask for forgiveness for all the things that 1 have thought, said and done today. Lord Jesus, 1 thank you that today 1 get an opportunity to stand before You Father God, 1 thank you for life, for health, for family.

Lord Jesus, 1 pray for marriages today; 1 pray that you will release marriages from the snares of hell. 1 pray that our jaded and broken unions will be resurrected and restored, Dear Lord. Lord Jesus, 1 pray that you would wage war against the devil and his principalities oh God. Jehovah, 1 call upon you

3

today and ask that you release your children from depression and suicidal thoughts in their marriages. I ask that you give them the strength, the power and the authority that I know has been delegated to all women in this world. Father God, You died on the cross so we can be free indeed; Lord Jesus release that resurrective power that married women forget that they have access to; the power that they gained when you were raised from the grave Oh God.

Lord Jesus, marriage is your sacred union; everyone who challenges this union must be rebuked; everyone who makes a mockery of this union is challenging You directly my Lord. We pray for such people Dear Lord, we forgive them because they lack understanding and Your guidance; we pray that You forgive them Lord because they are hurting, we pray Father God that you restore them.

Lord Jesus, batten down the foundations of our marriages, so that they serve You; release your supernatural power Lord Jesus, release Lord Jesus your wonder working power, release your miracle working power; let it fall and saturate Your people Lord Jesus; remove all the toxicity that is trying to kill the love you have manifested between two people. Resurrect their love Lord Jesus, release their love Father God, bless their dreams, bless their homes. And may your restorative blessings God, change their perspective of what life is, may they look at each other and see what You Father see in them, may they stop plotting and planning against one another my Lord, may they rather love and

4

hold on to each other and stand as one as promised. Lord I ask all these in Your glorious Holy name, Amen and amen.

Our reading today, reminds us of the power that we hold within us; the power of prayer and praise. We are reminded that when going through challenging times we must praise and pray; when things are incredible, we must praise and pray. Through praise, we soften Our Father's heart; our praises and prayers please Him. When God is pleased, He showers us with his love, He releases his abundant love; He releases healing; He releases miracles. His supernatural power to us feels like the roar of an earthquake. We are reminded that Our God's love transcends all, it shifts our foundations, and it is powerful enough to shake our environment. When your love shines on us, every one of our bands are loosed.

Psalm 91:1-4 "He that dwelleth in the secret place of the Most High Shall abide under the shadow of the Almighty. I will say of Jehovah, He is my refuge and my fortress; My God, in whom I trust. For he will deliver thee from the snare of the fowler, And from the deadly pestilence. He will cover thee with his pinions, And under his wings shalt thou take refuge: His truth is a shield and a buckler." Psalms 91:1-4 ASV Prayer Opener Father God in the name of Jesus Testimony On November 1,2019 God showed up and out in a mighty way. I was working in Ossining, NY. I am a medical examiner, which requires me to go to individuals place of business or their homes to perform medical exams on them for life insurance or disability insurance. I was driving on my way back to my office because it was the end of the day, so I have to spin blood, do paperwork, and ship out the kits for testing. I was on a

call to the office, Bluetooth of course up dating about cases that I completed that day. I came to a stop sign and told the office staff I was going to see her in about 20 minutes. I came to a complete stop because I was at stop sign. When I was pulling off from the corner of my eye to my right I saw a truck speeding and I was trying to move out of his way all I could do was brace myself for the impact. The car hit me dead on and my phone flew in the air. All of my airbags came out. The seatbelt pulled me back as the airbag hit me in my face so I really was dazed. I could not move or talk. I heard a lot of people screaming and yelling outside. I heard someone say she may be dead in there. I then started to realize what was going on. I then started looking at my arms and legs. I touched my face I didn't feel any blood, my nose wasn't broken from the force of the airbag. I can hear people asking if I was moving but I really at that time couldn't answer. I finally answered the phone because it was ringing off the hook. I was able to touch the screen on the car and I heard the girl at the office ask what happened because she heard the crash. I told her I was just hit by another car. She was trying to ask me where I was. I managed to tell her I was in Ossining but I really did not know where at in Ossining. She then explain my boss was on the way. I felt the tears rolled down my face because I knew the accident was bad. I could hear people asking if I was OK and not to move. Then I heard a gentleman come over and he said I saw the whole thing I know she has to be hurt. He then started trying to get into the car. The gentleman took out his knife and starting stabbing the airbags so he could hold my hand. 1 felt his warm hand which meant 1 had no nerve damage because i could touch and feel his hand so 1 believed. By this time the paramedics were on scene and they was explaining that 1 may have some broken bones or my back may be broken. 1 explained for them not to cut off my clothes. Finally when they opened the car door, by God's grace and mercy 1 walked out of the car! 1 walked out of the car. Besides the regular whip lash, nerve damage to my neck, God protected me because my work is not done. Thank you Jesus for your covering. By Author Pamela 1

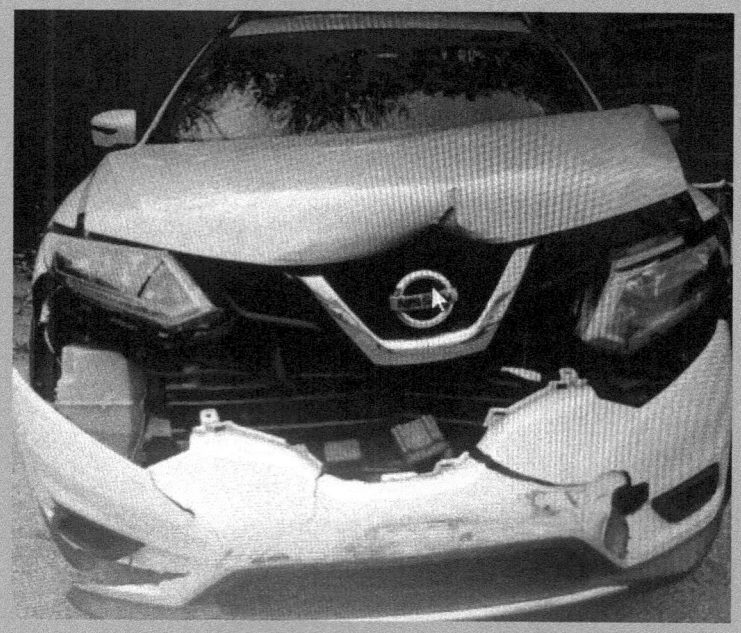

Minister Sherry Kirkland
He Will Never Leave Us Nor Forsake Us
(KJV) **Psalm 34:4** 4I sought the LORD, and he heard me, and delivered me from all my fears. One day, while scrolling through the internet, I came across some testimony videos. Videos of people who said that they had *found* God. That God had come into their lives in a powerful way, which resulted in their lives being changed forever. They spoke of a God that not only spoke to them, He heard them and responded to them. This was a concept that I wasn't familiar with. There was also a common thread throughout all their testimonies, each of these people claimed to have a relationship with God. Which was another idea that was foreign to me. I couldn't imagine having a personal relationship with God. I kept

watching testimony shows, and time and time again, I heard people talking about God like they really knew Him. I became fascinated with the idea that there was more to God than what I was experiencing. I wanted to know God like they did. If there was any chance that I could have a connection to the creator, I had to give it a try. The more curious I became about God, the more fearful I became about going to Hell. I was worried, afraid and I couldn't stop thinking about Hell. I had never had these feelings before. I attended church regularly but I was so unsure of where I stood with God. The possibility that I could spend eternity away from Him, began to weigh heavily on me. I knew I needed to talk to God.

At my church's next prayer service, I spoke to God from my heart. Actually, I was pleading with Him to not to let me end up in Hell. I begged Him to help me, to save me, to show me what to do. I felt like my heart was crying out to Him. And in the midst of my prayer, God gave me my first vision:

I could see a person in a hospital bed, from the waist down with a white sheet over them. The room was small. And leaning down from the ceiling with His right arm outstretched was Jesus.

Reaching down towards the person in the bed. This vision was amazing. It was a quick, clear flash but it was layered with information. It wasn't only what I saw, but what I knew and what I felt. These things together gave me a complete understanding of what God was telling me. I knew that the person was in a hospital room and I knew that the person in the bed was me, in my last moments of life. And I knew that Jesus was coming to take me home.

The understanding I received in that moment was that, we are not forsaken to Hell. That as long as there is breath in our bodies, we still have time to get it right. I was blown away because God had heard my cry, and responded to me.

This experience with God changed my life. I became determined to learn everything I could about God and to build my own relationship with Him. To use all the time that I have left, to get right with Him. God was right there, the whole time just waiting for me to turn to Him and to seek Him with my whole heart. I believe that God is waiting for each of us in the same way. I am still not sure if what I was shown was truly my last moments on Earth or just what I needed to see to get my life on track. But what I do know is that, that moment changed everything for me. My life has been full of His miracles, signs and wonders ever since. I just want everyone to know that God is never far from us, He is right there, all we have to do is turn Him with an open heart.

PRAYER:

Dear Lord Father God, thank you for loving us so much, thank you for being so faithful to your word and thank you for just being you. Lord we know that even when our eyes are not on you, that you are still right there. Father we ask that you open our hearts, open our minds, open our eyes and ears, so that we can see your truths and be drawn to them. We ask that you come into our lives, give us each an experience with you that changes our lives forever. We want a relationship with you Lord, we just need you to show us how. We want you to be our Father, our friend, our everything Lord. We love you, we praise you and we worship your Holy name. We ask all these things in the name of your son, Jesus Christ.

Amen

Title: Faith in Healing

Scripture Psalms46 :10   Be still and know that 1 am God:1 will be exalted among the heathen, 1 will be exalted in the earth.

During a health crisis 1 had to speak life over my situation.My dr gave me a prognosis. And while 1 was in the Dr office 1 said that 1 plead the blood of Jesus over the situation.And my health will be restore. 1 had to make a few changes my self.But 1 had faith it was going to be restored. HEBREWS 11:1(KJV)Now faith is the substance of things hoped

for,the evidence of things not seen.Even in darkness I
still believed. I told my Dr.my health will be restored
and started to praise the Lord in the Dr office. From
that moment. My health began to improve A few
months later I went back to my Dr.And there was
major improvement in my health.I felt it .I had faith of
God and I believed on His report .
This is why I will always have faith in healing.

Psalm 120:2

2 Save me , LORD, from lying lips and deceitful tongues.

       It was a hot Summer's night in June or July and I was working a fundraiser at the baseball stadium. One after the other I was checking out the excited and anxious baseball fans. Budweiser, hot dogs, and nachos were the items of choice at my register. One customer after the other, I would say, " thank you and enjoy the game." It was my mantra for the night.

       "Excuse me ma'am," a voice coming from my right said. As I turned around to see who it was reveal one of the ladies that could randomly check your register. Obviously at anytime. She took my register and asked me to step in the back with her. Mind you, I thought that she was just randomly

This really upset the big burly security guard. That I would not confess to something that I had not done. He told me let's go, he kept the tips that I had made that night, and walked me to the exit door. He and the lady that check my cash drawer, that was a penny over, told me that I could never come back to the stadium. It was those words that brought me to tears. I never really went to baseball games much but the thought of getting put out , told that I couldn't come back as well as humiliated proved to be too much at the moment. I began to cry.

After a few minutes I regained my composure and called my ride to come and get me. After I completed that call, I phoned the lady who facilitated the fundraiser and explained what happened. She was en route to the stadium. It seemed as though time stood still. I was so hurt that someone had excused me of stealing. After all, I was an educator and always strived to be an upstanding citizen in society. I reminded my self.

As I waited for my ride to come, I perused the area. People were coming and going. It was hustle and bustle. It was outside of the stadium in the downtown area. I turned to my right for about two seconds and when I turned back to my left, there was a man on a bicycle with a Lime Green t-shirt on. He asked me if I knew God. At this point I'm thinking what is really going on tonight? In a somewhat confused state I answered. I told him yes, I know God. He then extended his arm to hand me something. He said that God told him to give it to me. I'm reeling and still in an confused state thanked him. I didn't immediately look at what was given to me. Again I had just turned my head to my right for a second because I was looking for my ride and just wanted to go home. I looked back around to my left and the man on the bicycle with the Lime Green t-shirt on had vanished.

As quickly as the man appeared he disappeared. How could this be? The sidewalk was crowded with people. He was on a bike. It would have taken time to navigate thru all of them. And if nothing else, I would have seen his loud Lime Green t-shirt. So I finally look inside my hand to see what he had given me. It was a twenty-dollar bill! The exact same denomination that I was accused of stealing. It was a very surreal moment for me. I stood there awe struck. How could this be? The exact denomination that I was accused of stealing.

When I came to my senses, I immediately thanked the Most High. My father. I thanked the Most High, for knowing me. For knowing who I am and what I would not do. I thanked the Most High for letting me know that he was right there with me and had my back. I give all Honor, Praise, and Glory to the Most High.

Once the facilitator spoke to management, she called me later that evening and told me that I could go back to the stadium. Well, I was in no hurry to go checking my register. By this time she had use her walkie-talkie to summons security.

Now, I had asked what was going on. The lady said that she was requested to come to the counter to check my cash draw because I had stolen twenty- dollars from it and put it in my pant. pocket. I was dumbfounded. In total disbelief. I told the lady that I had done no such thing and IF I was going to steal it would at least be two-hundred dollars. Yes, it was a sarcastic remark, but it felt justifiable at the time because I was being condemned. I voluntarily pulled both pockets on my pants inside out. There was nothing. My shirt had no pockets on it. I would have taken off my shoes and socks if necessary to vindicated myself, but it was told to security that the twenty -dollars was in my pant pocket.

The both of them began to interrogate me as if we were taping an episode for Law and Order. They were trying to use reverse Psychology towards me to coerce me into agreeing to something that I was not guilty of. They grabbed my tip cup from off the counter and asked me how did I have so much money in my tip cup I told them that I was a professional and my goal was to provide quality service to their customers with a smile. Now I want you to keep in mind that this was a volunteer gig for a particular fundraiser. I stood my ground and didn't not let them move me, physically , mentally, emotionally, or spiritually.

there after what had just transpired. This incident happened years ago. The first time I stepped back in the stadium was last year. I was given a free ticket.

In conclusion, if there is anyone reading this devotional and don't truly believe that God is real or not right there beside you. I hope with all my heart that you will have a change of heart. Peace Be Unto You.

Pamela Hornsby-Irvin

Walking in Faith
Dr. Prophetess Sonya Gray

2 Corinthians 5:7-For we walk by faith, not by sight.
          Our goal is not to "finish first" in the race of
faith, but to reach out in a tangible way to
encourage others by setting an example and
lending a helping hand along the way to others.
This journey in life is a faith walk. In the Bible it
says, "for we walk by faith, not by sight" (2
Corinthians 5:7, KJV). We are to trust the Lord with
our whole heart and do not lean unto our own
understanding (Proverbs 3:5-6, KJV). What does it
really mean to trust God with your whole heart?

Can we truly put our everything in the hand of a person we have never seen? Sometimes we allow the thing of the world to stop our faith in God. We must not allow the things we go through to stop our faith walk. When we put our trust in God and allow Him to walk along side of us our faith increases. Let's walk by faith and trust God in this season of our lives. So, as you go about your life continue to walk by faith. Remember God's word strengthens our faith. We must do what God says in the word and stand strong in our faith, not wavering, for faith cometh by hearing and hearing by the word of God (2 Corinthians 5:17, KJV). We must let God do what is necessary in our lives so walk in faith every day. Prayer on Faith

Heavenly Father, at times I have no understanding where my life is concern. I seem to allow my life to spin out of control and allow situations to dictate my daily feelings. Give me the strength to walk in faith no matter what comes my way or what I face. The decisions that I need to make and choices that are in front of me. When obstacles seem hard, enemies come from all directions and I feel scared and alone walk with me as you strengthen my faith walk. Lord, you be the author and the finisher of my faith when I need it the most. In your matchless name I pray. Amen

Scriptures on Faith
Hebrews 11:6 Psalms 91:1-16
2 Corinthians 4:16-18 Hebrews 11:3
Romans 10:7
Hebrews 11:1-40
Romans 1:17
1 Peter 3:15
Ephesians 2:8-9
Romans 4:1-25

"Friendship"
Proverbs 17:17 ; Job 6:14 ; Luke 11:5-8

A man that hath friends must shew himself friendly; and there is a friend that sticketh closer than a brother. Proverbs 18:24 KJV

Society uses the term friendship loosely. Social Media web sites like Facebook connect us with many "friends" simultaneously; yet many of them are only acquaintances, not true friends.

The following passages reveals the meaning of a true friend. She is someone who brings out the best in you, who loves and gives unselfishly. She listens and speak the truth with kindness and when others criticize you she stands in your defense.

Friendship is never one sided because to have a

friend, we must be a friend. Think of your very best friend. Does she fit this description? Do you? And I say unto you, Ask, and it shall be given you; seek, and ye shall find; knock, and it shall be opened unto you.
for everyone that asketh receiveth; and he that seeketh findeth; and to him that knocketh it shall be opened.

Luke 11:9-10
A true friend is there through thick and thin, the good and the bad times. A true friend want ask the question "why" they will say when. If I have it, they can get it. Have you wakingy been in a situation where you feel like you are always giving? Feel like a one sided friendship, right? Just trust God that he will reveal to you if they are a true friend or an acquaintance.
Prayer:
Heavenly Father, Thank you for waking me up this morning clothed in my right mind. Lord, bless all those that stand in need of a blessing. Lord, continue to cover us, I give all praises to you, in Jesus name. Amen

Title: God is calling us

Scripture: Titus 2:3-5 New International Version (NIV)
3 Likewise, teach the older women to be reverent in the way they live, not to be slanderers or addicted to much wine, but to teach what is good. 4 Then they can urge the younger women to love their husbands and children, 5 to be self-controlled and pure, to be busy at home, to be kind, and to be subject to their husbands, so that no one will malign the word of God.

Why I decided to join this project and also write my book; my self journey with God.

My purpose which was established when God called me and wanted me to do serve his people. I remember the day so clearly. If only we would stop and listen to his message he would give us

in that toxic atmosphere and I was becoming toxic myself. After years of living angry, bitter, high strung, irritable and in denial that my controlling ways were deteriorating my body I ended up on a NYC Train having an anxiety attack. In that moment I lost control and couldn't go on; I called my Bishop and he prayed over me on that train until I got to the hospital. After I was admitted into the hospital I had to stay for a week. What got me here? I thought to myself.. Well, after working two jobs, 7 days a week, having no consistent relationship with Christ and keeping myself busy by plugging in people on to my calendar. God decided to force me to lay down. I was by myself in the hospital and not even capable to take a shower because my heart rate would not go lower than 145bpm. During those 7 days; God got my attention! I learned that only God can heal me and give me the strength to fight the enemy over my health. After several tests the doctors diagnosed me with sinus-tachycardia and if it's combined with anxiety then your heart rate will not be able to maintain a healthy steady heartbeat. I had to reflect on my personal life and schedule and put me first unless I would not be able to live a normal life. I had to study the word of God on Peace and listen to videos from Joyce Meyer, Marilyn Hickey and Joel Osteen. I literally moved out of New Jersey and went to a place where I only spent time outside in the nature. I took time for me and set healthy boundaries. I

memorized scriptures to help me mentally fight for my peace because no one could do it for me; other than the word of God and my inner strength to fight in the natural. The meaning of peace is: a state of tranquility and freedom from oppressive thoughts or emotions. In the fast pace life, we live in today with our cellphones, tablets, laptops, iphone watches, social media etc. there's no way to slow down. I was moving and grooving and when I did have time to unwind, I chose to fill my schedule with people. The problem with anxiety is that it's a disease that sneaks up without us being aware until we end up in the hospital or at the doctor's office. You see if our bodies don't get rest and we are always on the go and never enjoying the simple things in life; then we are overwhelmed with bills to pay for the things in our life and it robs our peace. The enemy seeks to destroy our peace, he doesn't care about your things, your job or your friends. He wants to invade your inner mind with feelings of not being enough and always having to do more, get more or to keep up with others that "seem" to have it all together. In order to keep your peace you must be at war daily using the word of God and setting healthy boundaries within yourself and family and friends.
Prayer Starter
Lord, Father, God thank you for being the Prince of Peace. Thank you for surrounding me with angels that protect my mind from false accusations from the devil.

I rebuke the enemy from my mind. I thank you Father for your peace that surpasses all understanding. I ask that the Holy Spirit give me the strength to overcome any fears in my heart. I thank you for protecting my Peace In Jesus Name I pray, AMEN!

AN ATTITUDE OF GRATITUDE

Scripture: Psalms 40:5 GNT : You have done many things for us, O LORD our God; there is no one like you! You have made many wonderful plans for us. I could never speak of them all--their number is so great!

Testimony: For most of my life, prayer had only been done in a reactive manner. I prayed when I was going through hard times or wanted to ask the Lord for something. As I grew stronger in my faith, I began to realize the importance of having a consistent prayer life.

I also realized that gratitude was the key to being consistent. Psalms 40:5, is the perfect example of the goodness of the Lord. It reminds us that he is always working things out on our behalf. Simply waking up every morning with breath in my lungs, is ALL the reason that I need to thank him and give him praise. I began to shift my prayer focus from what I wanted, to simply reverencing and honoring God for who he is.

Gratitude opens the door to finding and staying in your purpose. It opened my eyes to all that is good and caused me to find joy in new things. When I began to focus on that which is good, there was no time or room for negativity to occupy my mind.

Beginning everyday with a simple prayer of gratitude, changed my perspective and opened my eyes to truly seeing the goodness of the Lord. I began to think about God's grace and mercy, and ALL of the times he has loved me, even when I didn't love him (or myself). Starting my prayers with gratitude, shifted into more frequent prayers. I then, began to notice that I would pray more throughout the day and my relationship with God, began to get stronger.

My prayer life shifted from being a time of asking, to becoming a time of receiving. I began to actually seek the Lord. Seeking him required me to be still and listen. As I listened, I began to recognize his voice and hear it more clearly. Having a consistent and meaningful prayer life can also be yours. I challenge you to begin to develop an attitude of gratitude. You will see that you have a lot to be thankful for. Whenever a negative thought tries to enter your mind, combat it with a praise unto the Lord. Allow your praise to be your weapon and you will the walls in your life begin to crumble.

The enemy wants to occupy our mind and cause anxiety or depression to dwell within. Choose, to think on those things which are good, and watch the transformation that takes place within your life. God wants more for us than we can ever think or imagine. When you allow him to be the center of your joy, your perspective will begin to shift and everything that is not in alignment with his perfect plan will be dismantled.

From this day forward, choose you and choose to be happy. Begin to take everything before the Lord in prayer and he will show you the way. Seek his voice by reading and meditating on his word and he will reveal things to you that was once hidden. His word in Jeremiah 29:11, says that he has plans to prosper us. Believe that word and walk boldly knowing that he is on your side and you will not fail. Allow gratitude to lead you into a stronger relationship with God and remember the he will never leave no forsake you.

Prayer Starter: Heavenly Father, I come to you with a grateful heart. Not to ask you for anything, but to simply say "Thank You. Thank you for everything that you have already done. I count it not lightly that you continue to love and protect me. Thank you for your continuous grace and mercy, even during the times that I did not deserve it. Thank you for ordering my steps and opening my eyes to your perfect plan.

Lord, thank for revealing to me my God-given purpose and for opening the doors to do your will. Let me always rejoice in you and have an everlasting peace that surpasses all understanding. Open the eyes of my heart to see that which you will have me to see. Remove anything that distracts me from being in your will. Restore a spirit of joy in my heart and let me continuously speak life.

I declare that I shall walk in victory and your praises shall continually be in my mouth. I decree that from this day forward, I will always see the beauty in that which you have created. Continue to reveal to me the plan that you have ordered and let me forever walk with clarity, boldness and authority. I thank you and I praise you. It is in the mighty name of Jesus that I pray, Amen.

PEACE IN THE MIDST OF IT ALL.

TESTIMONY:
My peace I have during the Corona Virus.
SCRIPTURE:
PHILIPPIANS 4:6-7
BE CAREFUL FOR NOTHING BUT IN EVERY THING
BY PRAYER AND SUPPLICATION WITH
THANKSGIVING LET YOUR REQUEST BE KNOWN
UNTO GOD AND THE PEACE THAT SURPASSES ALL
UNDERSTANDING SHALL KEEP YOUR HEARTS AND
MINDS .

Dear father God give those peace in their
minds dealing with trials and tribulations. Please
teach them to depend on you. Please grant them
peace that is unexplainable. Grant them the peace to
rest in your arms.
As the scripture say in John 14:27 Peace I leave with
you my peace I give you I do not give you as the

world. Do not let your heart be troubled
Lord please give peace with those who have internal
conflicts from society such as depression and
forgiveness and the cares of society.Please give
those peace that their sins are counted and covered
in the blood of Jesus.Let your lasting peace be built
on your people and let there be no room for doubt
or fear.I pray every one be strengthened in peace.I
pray for peace for those who trespass ed against
them .May every one have peace through the fruit if
that spirit and every one hold peace in their faith.
WHEN YOU REST IN HIS ARMS IN THE MIDST OF IT
ALL YOU WILL HAVE PEACE IN EVERY THING,   BE
ENCOURAGED, BE STRENGTHENED AND MOST
IMPORTANTLY BE BLESSED.   AMEN.

Walk in Peace
Dr. Prophetess Sonya Gray

2 Corinthians 13: 11- Finally, brethren, farewell. Be perfect, be of good comfort, be of one mind, live in peace; and the God of love and peace shall be with you.

When I think of peace I remember when Jesus sent out His disciples two by two to preach and heal. We as Kingdom citizens are to go into our cities and town telling the people, "Peace be unto you." How can we live in peace when we don't apply the word of God to our lives? For years I had no peace and I lived with strongholds from previous relationships. Then one day I found a man who sticks closer than a brother every day. His name was Jesus. He has been my everything since I was three years old and he has kept me through no must. Jesus has been a present help in the time of trouble. God has been with me through everything that the enemy threw at me and he has kept me in perfect peace. I am thankful to have a relationship with God now and because of having an authentic relationship I can work in a peace like a river today. As you walk in peace know that God is walking with you daily. He is the peace that moves mountains and will keep you daily.

Prayer for Peace

Heavenly Father, please grant me peace of mind and calm my troubled heart. Lord keep my soul from trouble. May I always be at peace. May you grant me awareness of myself. May you heal my body and I have peace as well as be a source of healing to others when they need peace. May the peace of God dwell in us always in the mighty name of Jesus. Amen

Scriptures on Peace

2 Thessalonians   3:16 Hebrews 12:14
John 16:33   1 Peter 5: 6-7
Philippians4:6   Psalms 4:8
Isaiah 26:3   Proverbs 12:20
1 Peter 5:7   Isaiah 12:2
Matthew 10:34-36   1 Corinthians 14:33
1 Peter 3:11   Romans 15:13

Mabakuena Khalema
Maseru, Lesotho

Pamela J Hayes-
Liggins
New York, NY

Sherry Kirkland
Anderson SC

Pamela Horsnby-Irvin
St Louis Missouri

Diana Hill
Philadelphia, PA

Dr. Sonya R Gray
Moore SC

C. Annette Reynolds
Myrtle Beach SC

Julie Thomas
Detroit Michigan

Angelique Avendano

Kesha Tilton

Journal Pages

Journal Pages

Journal Pages

Journal Pages

Journal Pages

Journal Pages

_____

_____

_____

_____

_____

_____

_____

_____

_____

_____

_____

_____

_____

Journal Pages

Journal Pages

_____

_____

_____

_____

_____

_____

_____

_____

_____

_____

_____

_____

_____

Journal Pages

Journal Pages

Journal Pages

Lightning Source UK Ltd.
Milton Keynes UK
UKHW022047140620
364909UK00004B/682